THE BIBLE
OF THE
EVANGELICAL
CHURCH

David F. Wells

THE BANNER OF TRUTH TRUST

THE BANNER OF TRUTH TRUST
3 Murrayfield Road, Edinburgh EH12 6EL
P.O. Box 621, Carlisle, Pennsylvania 17013, USA

*

© The Banner of Truth Trust 1995
First Published 1995
ISBN 0 85151 682 3

*

Typeset in 10½/12pt Plantin Monotype
Printed in Great Britain by
Howie and Seath Ltd, Edinburgh

I came to America twenty-five years ago, a newly minted doctor and ready to begin a teaching ministry. Today I look back on this quarter of a century with immense gratitude. America is, indeed, a land of milk and honey and I am grateful for the opportunity to serve Christ during these years and for the nourishment which I have received from the Church during this time.

This quarter of a century has been a time of many bright highlights, but if I am not mistaken it is also a time of lengthening shadows in our evangelical world. We have been transformed from being an inconsequential religious player to one of some consequence during this time, but the costs are now becoming plain.

Twenty-five years ago, evangelicals were outside the religious establishment. That establishment was made up principally of the mainline denominations. But today evangelicals have become the religious establishment, however informally. But despite this, I believe that today we are in some peril. We have a fight on our hands and what we're fighting for is our evangelical soul, for it is possible for us to gain the whole religious world while losing our own souls. I do not say this because I am one of those who thinks that the best is always what is in the past, that we are always in a state of decline, and that if we want to think of a golden age we have to think of something that is behind us. I do not think that way at all. In some ways we, today, are better off than we were twenty-five years ago. Perhaps a lot better off. And yet in spite of that, I believe there are matters within the evangelical world today which are seriously amiss.

So what I would like to do in the time that I have is to look, first, at some of the great surface changes which have taken place during this time and, second, I want to try to look beneath the surface of those changes, and then, third, I want to begin sketching out ways in which I think we might seek to change some directions. So what is the peril I see happening?

Change on the Surface
What has changed most dramatically, I believe, in this last quarter of a century is that when I first arrived here we were at the end of the post war period when evangelical faith was being *doctrinally* framed and today, for the most part, it is not. Or at least, not obviously so. What shaped the Church then, far more than it does now, was theological conviction about its character and purpose. What shapes it now, far more than it did then, is a *marketing ethos*. In one sense, this should not be surprising at all. Americans are nothing if not consumers, consumers of images, of relationships, and of things. You perhaps will have seen some of these figures that have been assembled in recent years. We have 7% of the world's population but we consume 33% of the goods and services. Every year in America, 12 billion catalogues are sent out to see if some unwary consumers can be attracted. The average child watches 20 thousand advertisements on television every year and on an average day you should see 1,600 advertisements. Our whole society has been transformed into a consumer's heaven and we are nothing if not a nation of buyers, thoroughly at home in, and thoroughly a part of, the life of commerce. We move in and out of it much like fish do through water. It is in this commerce that

we live and move and have our being. So the Church's willingness to adapt to the marketing model for thinking about itself really is not remarkable.

But in adapting itself to this culture, the Church, far more than was the case twenty-five years ago, is having its character, and its purposes, and the way it functions, defined for it. There's nothing wrong with commerce *per se,* but I am going to argue that there is something profoundly wrong in trading Christ, or in thinking that religion is the commerce of the soul. Now this adaptation to this kind of culture I see taking place in three very important ways in the evangelical world.

First, the churches, in larger and larger numbers, are adapting themselves to felt needs in their congregations much as a business might adapt its product to a market. In other words, the Church is sanctioning the idea that when someone comes in its doors it's okay to view that person as a consumer, somebody who is going to attempt to hitch up a product to their own felt needs. The products in question, of course, are the activities, the experiences, the amenities, and the message of the Church. However, what people who are coming in these church doors today are thinking about, and what they want, is not primarily personal salvation. What they want is a sense of *personal well-being,* however momentary and fragmentary that personal sense of well-being is and our churches are beginning to cater to this. I have no doubt at all that they are going to become very successful. Indeed, some are successful already and they are going to become more successful because marketing in America is what makes the wheels go around. They are, in other words, simply doing what Pepsi has done, what self-help groups have done, the auto makers, the makers of jeans, the makers of movies, and what Madonna herself has done. So why shouldn't churches do this, somebody might ask? Why shouldn't they want to be successful in the same way that Pepsi and Madonna are?

The answer is that marketing will produce success but not necessarily the kind that has much to do with the Kingdom of God. To start with, the analogy between the business world and the world of Christ's Kingdom is a completely fallacious analogy. Consumers in the market place are never asked to commit themselves to the product they are purchasing as a sinner is to the Christ in whom belief is being invited. Furthermore, consumers in the marketplace are free to define their needs however they want to and then to hitch up a product to satisfy those needs, but in the Church the consumer, the sinner, is not free to define his or her needs exactly as they wish. It is *God* who defines our needs and the reason for that is that left to ourselves we would not understand our needs aright because we are rebels against God. We are hostile both to God and to His law and cannot be subject to either, Paul tells us. Now, no person going into the marketplace, going to buy a coffee-pot or going to buy a garden hose, engages with their innermost being in the way that we are inviting sinners to do in the Church. The analogy is simply fallacious.

Furthermore, we would be wise to remember that it was the Liberal Protestants who equated cultural success with the Kingdom of God. In their case, they equated cultural success with the place where the Kingdom of God was coming into being in *high* culture. We are wanting to equate marketing success with the place where the Kingdom of God is coming into being in *popular* culture. Our immediate forebears in the faith, however, those who pioneered evangelical faith after World War II, resisted this connection between the Kingdom of God and success. We would be wise if we did the same. For what succeeds in this world is not necessarily what is true or what is right.

Indeed, much that is false and decadent succeeds. A Church, if it is really true to itself, is never going to be a worldly success. Its gospel is stupid. Many, we know, are called but few are chosen. Much seed is sown, but only a little produces a rich harvest. And when Christ returns is he going to find faith on the face of the earth? Is it right, then, for the Church to prostrate itself obsequiously before the world in this sorry quest to become a going and successful enterprise? Is it right to allow sinners, hostile in their nature both to God and His law, to define how the Church is going to do its business? I think not. So this is the first place where I see our habits as consumers entering into our world and defining how we function.

There is a second place that the intrusion of the market ethos into the life of a church is having a profound effect on the way that the ministry is understood and practised. During the last fifty years in particular, the ministry has become increasingly *professionalized*. Indeed, it is not coincidental that during this time, when the social status of ministers has declined, the need for them to see themselves as professionals has increased. By professionalization, I simply mean that ministers are being driven to understand themselves as specialists, those who have a special kind of knowledge, the same way lawyers and physicians and chemists do. In these other professions, specialized knowledge is used in the pursuit of acquisition and aspiration. That is to say, professionals typically have careers, projectories of accomplishment for which planning and manoeuvring are indispensable. Where this enters the Church and where ministers begin to think of themselves in these terms, an ethos results which I believe is extremely harmful to the real interests of the Church. What happens, amongst other things, as ministers begin to nourish and pursue private careers is that the older virtues that were once thought to be essential to the ministry are replaced by some new virtues. The importance of theology is eclipsed by the clamor for management skills, biblical preaching by entertaining story-telling, godly character by engaging personality, and the work of the ministry by the art of sustaining a career. I believe that these are all unhappy exchanges.

There is a third place where the marketing ethos is entering. The recasting of religion in terms of the market is giving entrepreneurs a field day. In 1970, apart from the National Association of Evangelicals and *Christianity Today,* some missions organizations, some colleges and seminaries, and the religious presses, there were virtually no evangelical organizations at all. Today, if you consult Melton's *Directory of Religious Organizations in America,* you will be dumbfounded to find that probably between 40% to 50% of all religious organizations are evangelical and virtually all of them have been started since 1970. They are now outflanking the churches and denominations. It needs to be said immediately, of course, that many of these organizations are exercising very fine ministries and many are doing the work that the churches have not been able to do. At the same time, however, where the market principle is at work, there you will get entrepreneurs and though entrepreneurs have great ability in getting things started, it is also the case that sometimes if entrepreneurs are not careful what they build is also their own personal fiefdoms. And some of the noise that you hear in the evangelical world today is the noise of competing personal empires. This is what shocks Christians who come from the Third World. It shocks them! This was the theme that came up repeatedly at Lausanne II, the International Congress on World Evangelization that was held in Manila in 1989. They could not understand how we tolerate this. Competition fuelled by personal ambition destroys the co-operation that should grow from our common ownership by Christ. 'It is a jungle out there,' we say of the corporate world. It is also a jungle out there in the evangelical world.

So, let me sum up. The market, as I understand it, is affecting both the internal ethos in the Church and its external organization. Internally, it is inclining us to think of sinners as consumers and it is driving ministers to think of themselves as professionals who have personal careers to nourish, so they are not slow to pick up their belongings and take to the road to find better opportunities. And the market is changing the external structures of evangelicalism, most obviously by encouraging us to think that religion provides us with a field of opportunity. As significant as these things are, however, they are just the surface changes and it is what lies beneath this that is of rather more interest to me.

Changes Below the Surface

In 1993 a very interesting study was done which revisited George Gallup's figure of 32% of adult Americans who claim to be reborn. What this study did was to add just a few modest tokens of commitment as additional tests. In addition to asking, 'Are you born again?,' they also asked, 'Do you go to church with some regularity, do you pray with some regularity, and do you have some minimal structure of formal Christian belief?' When those tests were added, the figure of 32% dropped to 8%. And if we were to probe just a little bit more, and if we were to ask: first, 'Are you regenerate?'; second, 'Do you have a sufficiently cogent worldview to make a difference in society?'; and third, 'Do you have a sufficiently formed Christian character to want to do so?', based on some ongoing research I have seen, my guess is that the figure may be no more than 1% or 2%. What this means, my brothers and sisters, is that we may have been living in a fool's paradise. When Gallup produced his figures in the 1970s, and has repeated them every year ever since, it seemed like evangelicals were on a roll with such wide popular support and with churches that were growing. It looked as though we were on the verge of sweeping all of our religious and cultural opponents before us. That was why these figures stirred such alarm in the secular media, why they created some heartburn in the mainline Protestant denominations, and why they produced just a little power-mongering amongst evangelicals. But it has turned out to be an optical illusion. The reality that we have to face today is that we have produced a plague of *nominal evangelicalism* which is as trite and as superficial as anything we have seen in Catholic Europe.

Now, why is this? Well, I would like to suggest that it begins with the crumbling of our theological character. I have spoken of this in my book, *No Place for Truth*, in terms of the 'disappearance of theology.' It is not that theological beliefs are denied, but that they have little cash value. They don't matter. I likened the situation to that of a child who is in a home but who is ignored. It is not that the child has been abducted; the child is there. The child is in the home, but has no legitimate place in the family. And, again, research which I have had conducted strongly points to the fact that where this kind of theological character is crumbling, there the centrality of God is disappearing. God now comes to rest lightly and inconsequentially upon the Church. This, however, is just our own private, evangelical version of what we see more generally in the culture. In the broader culture we learn that 91% of people say that God is very important to them but 66% go on to say that they do not believe in moral absolutes, and 67% do not believe in absolute truth. So God rests inconsequentially upon their lives.

An evangelical faith that is not passionate about truth

and righteousness is a faith which is a lost cause. All that it will then be living for is simply its own organizational preservation. Last century William James saw this same sort of mindset at work. The entire modern deification of survival, he said, 'with the denial of any semblance of excellence in what survived, except the capacity for more survival still, is surely the strangest intellectual stopping place ever.' Stanley Fish, the radical deconstructionist, in his latest book says that since there is no such thing as truth, all that we have left is power, politics, and persuasion. Given his premise, he is right and I can tell you that if we do not recover our theological character and our sense of truth, in the same way, all that we are going to have left is power, politics, and persuasion. Those will be the only means we will be left for survival. If this is an accurate analysis, where are we going to start in finding some new directions?

In a recent book, *The Churching of America: Winners and Losers in the Religious Economy*, Fink and Stark developed an interesting thesis. Just as there is commercial economy, they say, so there is a religious economy. That is to say, there are cultural circumstances which encourage the success of some religious movements and discourage the success of others. I think that they are right. However, there is one small section of that book that seems to have been overlooked. What they say here is that regardless of how much success the culture bestows upon a religious movement, it will never survive long term unless it has what they call, 'a vivid other worldliness.' Without looking at evangelicals directly, they have in actual fact put their finger on our Achilles heel, for amidst all of the abundance in our world, all of the accoutrements that go with a successful movement, a vivid other worldliness is often conspicuous by its absence. If we cannot reverse ourselves at this point, we are headed towards the oblivion of irrelevance before

[9]

God. So how are we going to recover a vivid other world-liness? Perhaps it consists in many things, but I single out just two which I think are central.

The Lost Word

First, we must recover the lost Word of God. The problem is not, of course, that the Bible itself has disappeared. There are, in fact, enough Bibles in America to put one in every home. No, the problem is that we are not *hearing* the Word of God. It does not rest consequentially upon us. It does not cut. And it is surely one of the great ironies of our time that in the 1970s and 80s so much effort was put into defining inspiration and looking at what were the best words to express and protect it. And while all of that work was going on, unnoticed by us, the Church was quietly unhitching itself from the truth of Scripture in *practice*. Biblical inspiration was affirmed but its consequences were not worked out for our preaching, our techniques for growing the Church, our techniques for healing our own fractured selves. These all happened largely without the use of Scripture. It is as if we think that while the Bible is inspired, it is nevertheless inadequate to the tasks of sustaining and nourishing the twentieth-century Church! It is almost as if God, when he inspired the Word could not see what was coming in the late twentieth century! The result of this divine myopia is that he has left us with something that is inadequate to the great challenges that we face today.

If we do not recover the sufficiency of the Word of God in our time, if we do not relearn what it means to be sustained by it, nourished by it, disciplined by it, and unless our preachers find the courage again to preach its truth, to allow their sermons to be defined by its truth, we will lose our right to call ourselves Protestants, we will lose our capacity to be the people of God, and we will set ourselves on a path that leads right into the old discredited liberal Protestantism. We have to recover a vivid other worldliness by making ourselves once again captives to the truth of God regardless of the cultural consequences. So that is the first thing.

The Lost Vision

Second, it will be impossible to recover a vivid other world-liness without recovering a fresh vision of God as *holy*. We, today, are actually on the verge of a fresh theological discovery of a very different kind. It is that God is centrally love and that he is only peripherally and remotely holy. And in so doing we are on the verge of standing Scripture on its head. No, the holiness of God is not peripheral. It is central, and without this holiness our faith loses its meaning entirely. As P. T. Forsyth declared a century ago, 'sin is but the defiance of God's holiness, grace is but its action upon sin, the cross is but its victory, and faith is but its worship.' And so without a compelling vision of the holiness of God, worship inevitably loses its awe, the truth of God's Word loses its interest, obedience loses its virtue, and the Church loses its moral authority. And it is precisely here that modernity, which is more or less synonymous with 'the world' in the New Testament, has made its deepest intrusion into the life of the Church. Modernity has rearranged our appetites.

Because of our therapeutic culture, we favor relational matters over those that are moral, the consequence of which is that God's holiness is pushed into the background and his love is brought into the foreground. Mysticism then flourishes and cognitive conviction retreats. Self-surrender is devalued and self-fulfillment is prized. Preoccupation with character fades and fascination with personality and self-image advance. The God in whom love has replaced wrath produces a Christianity that is appealing for its civility, but one that has no serious Word for a world which is racked by evil. It is a form of belief that is sympathetic but not searching, that lends its ear but not its revelation of the Holy One. Without the holiness of God, sin is just failure – but not failure before God! It is failure without the presumption of guilt, without retribution, indeed without any serious moral meaning at all. And without the holiness of God, grace is no longer grace. It is not grace from God, grace from the God who, against his own holy nature, has reconciled sinners to himself in Christ. And without justification there is no gospel and without the gospel, there is no Christianity. So if we lose sight of the holiness of *God*, we lose sight of entire faith and we lose the right to call ourselves Protestants in any recognizably historical sense.

Until this is seen afresh, until it enters the very innermost fibers of our being, our virtue is going to be without seriousness, our believing without gravity, our practice without moral pungency, our worship without joyful seriousness, and our preaching without power. And without these virtues, these virtues of an historic Protestant faith, the Church today is simply going to become just one more special interest in a world that is awash with special interests. Modernity will not have its power to rearrange our inner lives destroyed. What is most lost is what most needs to be recovered. It is the unsettling, disconcerting, moral presence of God in our midst. He can no longer be the junior partner in our religious enterprises and he can never be just an ornamental decoration upon our Church life. It is because God now rests so inconsequentially upon the Church that the Church is free to plot and to devise its success in its own way. That is why so many of our forebears in the faith would scarcely even recognize us as their children today.

Today, the evangelical world is bleeding. We have lived

off the accumulated capital of those who worked so hard in post-War years and we have not renewed it. Fifty-one years ago, Harold John Ockenga addressed the National Association of Evangelicals when it was very much in its infancy. He spoke of the crisis in Western civilization and of the responsibilities evangelicals had. Let me quote from his address: 'This nation in its maturity,' he said, 'is passing through a crisis which is enmeshing western civilization. Confusion exists on every hand. We are living in a very difficult and bewildering time, but few people realize what tremendous change we are undergoing.' And he continued, 'The hour has arrived when the people of this nation must think deeply or be damned. We must recognize that we are standing at the cross-roads and that there are only two ways that lie open before us. One is the road of the rescue of Western civilization by a re-emphasis on the revival of evangelical Christianity. The other is a return to the dark ages of heathendom, which powerful force is emerging in every phase of our lives today.' Those were prophetic words and if I am not mistaken, we, today, despite all of our prosperity, have little left of what it takes to impact our secular world. That is the irony of our success!

And so may God give us the willingness to repent where we must and may he give us again the desire to think large thoughts of him and his truth. And may he enable us to disengage our faith from the culture in order that we might freshly re-engage the culture out of a passionate concern for truth and righteousness. This is a time when we can seek again the grace of God to these ends. Let us seek his grace so that the evangelicalism that we leave behind, that which the coming generation sees, is one that is filled with the excellence of the knowledge of God. Amen.

Other booklets in this series:

The Authentic Gospel, *Jeffrey E. Wilson*
Behind a Frowning Providence, *John J. Murray*
Biblical Church Discipline, *Daniel Wray*
The Carnal Christian, *E. C. Reisinger*
Christians Grieve Too, *D. Howard*
Coming to Faith in Christ, *John Benton*
The Cross - The Vindication of God, *D. M. Lloyd-Jones*
The Five Points of Calvinism, *W. J. Seaton*
Healthy Christian Growth, *Sinclair B. Ferguson*
Holiness, *Joel R. Beeke*
The Importance of The Local Church, *D. Wray*
The Incomparable Book, *W. McDowell*
The Invitation System, *Iain H. Murray*
Is There an Answer? *Roger Ellsworth*
A Life of Principled Obedience, *A. N. Martin*
Living the Christian Life, *A. N. Martin*
The Moral Basis of Faith, *Tom Wells*
Open Your Mouth for the Dumb, *Peter Barnes*
Origins? *R.B. Ranganathan*
The Practical Implications of Calvinism, *A. N. Martin*
Read Any Good Books?, *Sinclair B. Ferguson*
Reading the Bible, *Geoffrey Thomas*
Seeing Jesus, *Peter Barnes*
Victory: The Work of the Spirit, *P. Potgieter*
What is the Reformed Faith, *J. R. de Witt*
What's Wrong With Preaching Today?, *A. N. Martin*

For free illustrated catalogue please write to
THE BANNER OF TRUTH TRUST 3 Murrayfield Road,
Edinburgh EH12 6EL
P O Box 621, Carlisle, Pennsylvania 17013, U.S.A.